HALLOWEEN PARTY FAVORS: I SPY HALLOWEEN BOOK FOR KIDS AGES 2-5

A Fun Activity Book with Spooky Guessing Games for Toddlers, Preschool & Kindergarten | Halloween Gifts for Kids

Halloween is a thrilling and spooky holiday, celebrated with a sense of mystery and excitement. It's a time when ghosts and ghouls come out to play, and tales of the supernatural send shivers down your spine. In eerie decorations and the hunt for delicious treats, Halloween is a celebration of all things spooky and mysterious.

So, who's up for a spine-tingling Halloween adventure with this book?

HOW TO PLAY:

Look at the creepy and eerie pictures and find the item that matches the spooky letter given. Turn to the next page to reveal the answer to the mysterious riddle. Prepare your coloring supplies, and may the Halloween spirits be with you!

I SPY with my little eye something beginning with...

BAT

CAT

I SPY with my little eye something beginning with...

DRACULA

EYEBALL

FANGS

I SPY with my little eye something beginning with...

GHOST

HAT

IMP

JACK-O-LANTERN

KNIFE

I SPY with my little eye something beginning with...

LOLLIPOP

I SPY with my little eye something beginning with...

MUMMY

I SPY with my little eye something beginning with...

NECKLACE

I SPY with my little eye something beginning with...

PUMPKIN

I SPY with my little eye something beginning with...

QUEEN

I SPY with my little eye something beginning with...

REAPER

SKULL

TOMATO

I SPY with my little eye something beginning with...

UMBRELLA

WITCH

X-RAY CAT

YETI

I SPY with my little eye something beginning with...

ZOMBIE

Made in the USA
Las Vegas, NV
10 October 2023

78904097R00063